NEW HAMPSHIRE

NEW HAMPSHIRE

Dottie Brown

Lerner Publications Company

LIBRARY OF CONGRESS
CATALOGING-IN-PUBLICATION DATA
Brown, Dottie.
    New Hampshire / Dottie Brown.
        p.   cm. — (Hello USA)
    Includes index.
    Summary: Introduces the geography, history, people, industries, and environmental concerns of the Granite State.
    ISBN 0–8225–2730–8 (lib. bdg.)
    1. New Hampshire – Juvenile literature.
[1. New Hampshire.] I. Title. II. Series.
F34.3.B76   1993
974.2 – dc20   92–31057
                                           CIP
                                            AC

CURR
F
34.3
.B76
1993

Manufactured in the United States of America

1   2   3   4   5   6   98   97   96   95   94   93

Cover photograph by Craig Blouin.

The glossary on page 69 gives definitions of words shown in **bold type** in the text.

 This book is printed on acid-free, recyclable paper.

CONTENTS

Did You Know . . . ?

❑ In 1934 workers at Mount Washington's weather observatory in New Hampshire witnessed the most powerful gust of wind ever recorded on land. The wind speed was measured at 231 miles (372 kilometers) per hour.

❑ More people have climbed Mount Monadnock in New Hampshire than any other mountain in North America.

Portsmouth

❏ In 1800 the U.S. Navy chose the harbor at Portsmouth, New Hampshire, for its first official naval shipyard.

❏ Skiing has long been a big part of New Hampshire's winters. The state boasts the nation's first ski club (1872), first ski school (1929), first cleared ski trail (1930), and first overhead tow (1935).

❏ On January 5, 1776, New Hampshire became the first of the 13 colonies to declare its independence from Great Britain.

7

Old Man of the Mountains

A Trip Around the State

Perched atop one of New Hampshire's many rocky peaks, the Old Man of the Mountains overlooks the countryside. Huge granite rocks collided thousands of years ago and shaped the figure, also known as Great Stone Face. Over time, people living in the area have passed along stories about the face. Great Stone Face has become part of the reason for New Hampshire's nickname —the Granite State.

Granite—a hard rock known for its strength and beauty—is a symbol of New Hampshire. The state's many mountains and hills are filled with granite. Thick, green forests cover most of the Granite State's rocky landscape.

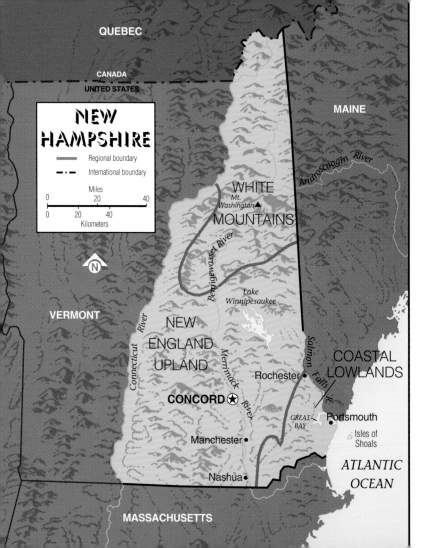

New Hampshire is shaped like a skinny triangle. Massachusetts forms the base of the triangle, and Canada borders the northern tip. Vermont is New Hampshire's neighbor to the west. Maine and the Atlantic Ocean border New Hampshire on the east.

Nestled in the northeastern corner of the United States, New Hampshire is part of New England. Fire and ice sculpted the land long before people ever lived in New Hampshire. More than 100 million years ago, pressures inside the earth forced **lava,** or blazing, melted rock, up to the earth's surface. As time passed, the rock hardened in slabs. **Glaciers**—huge, solid sheets of ice—moved across the rocky land millions of years later.

As they pushed south, the glaciers shaped much of the land in the Granite State by carving valleys, grinding down mountains, and scooping out earth to form lake beds. By the time the glaciers melted, they had molded three land regions in what is now New Hampshire—the Coastal Lowlands, the New England Upland, and the White Mountains.

Granite wall

The Coastal Lowlands cover the southeastern corner of New Hampshire and stretch about 20 miles (32 km) inland from the Atlantic Ocean. Sandy beaches blanket parts of the region's winding shoreline. Portsmouth, which lies near the coast, is the state's only shipping port.

Known for its many lakes, trees, and rolling hills, the New England Upland extends over the rest of the southern half of the state. Some of New Hampshire's most fertile farmland lies in the region. And much of the state's granite is mined in the New England Upland, near the city of Concord.

Offshore islands (left) **are part of the Coastal Lowlands. Farmland** (right) **covers much of the New England Upland. Storms can form quickly over the White Mountains** (far right).

The White Mountain region extends north of the New England Upland. Tall mountains cover most of the region, but the slopes flatten out near the Canadian border. Six peaks in the White Mountains, all named after U.S. presidents, rise more than one mile (1.6 km) into the sky.

High in the White Mountains, many streams begin their tumbling course down the slopes. The Pemigewasset River forms here, near the Old Man of the Mountains, and flows south into the Merrimack River.

The Connecticut River, which begins near the northern tip of the state, separates New Hampshire from Vermont. The Androscoggin River rushes through thick forests in northeastern New Hampshire before entering Maine. Many small rivers and streams flow into Great Bay, a large body of salt water connected to the Atlantic Ocean by the Piscataqua River.

New Hampshire has many lakes —about 1,300 in all. The largest lakes, including Winnipesaukee

Pemigewasset River

and Squam, lie in the New England Upland. Near the state's northern boundary, the Connecticut Lakes lead up into Canada.

The Atlantic Ocean creates a big difference between the climate near New Hampshire's coast and

that of the rest of the state. In the winter, the ocean holds in heat and keeps the air fairly warm near the coast, where temperatures hover around 25° F (–4° C). But higher up, in the White Mountains, the air can be chilling. Here, the temperature can plunge far below zero (–18° C). New Hampshire's summers tend to be dry and cool, with temperatures averaging about 70° F (21° C).

Most of New Hampshire's **precipitation** (rain and melted snow) comes in the form of snow. More than 100 inches (254 centimeters) of snow fall in the mountains each year, but the coast gets much less. In the summer, most parts of the state receive 10 to 15 inches (25 to 38 cm) of rain.

The loon patrol looks out for the safety of New Hampshire's large diving birds.

Rain and melted snow provide plenty of water for New Hampshire's trees. More than 85 percent of the state is wooded. Oak, sugar maple, beech, and birch trees grow alongside pines, spruces, and cedars. Flowering shrubs, violets, and fireweeds add color to the state's landscape. New Hampshire's state flower, the purple lilac, blossoms in the lowlands.

The state's woodlands are home to many kinds of animals. Black bears roam far in the north, where moose feed on shrubs and water plants. Deer, chipmunks, mink, and foxes scamper throughout the state's countryside. Near lakeshores, loons, ducks, and geese nest. Coastal waters shelter lobsters, oysters, and shrimp.

A moose *(above)* **peers through the trees, and a curious fox pup** *(inset)* **awaits its mother.**

For centuries, the rivers and lakes in the area that became New Hampshire provided American Indians with plenty of fish.

New Hampshire's Story

The first people to live near the Atlantic coast were American Indians, or Native Americans, who settled in the area thousands of years ago. By the year A.D. 1500, the Pennacook—who were descendants of the earliest Indians— were the main tribe living in the woodlands of what is now New Hampshire. The Pennacook and neighboring Indians shared similar customs and understood each other's languages.

Pennacook villages housed 50 to 200 people. Families lived in dome-shaped wigwams, which the women built. They made frames from the branches of young, flexible trees and covered the frames with bark. To keep warm in the winter, the Indians lined the walls of the wigwams with fur.

Children played with dolls
made from corn husks and
corn silk.

Pennacook women also farmed
small plots of land, growing pumpkins, squashes, beans, and corn.
With their children, the women
gathered strawberries, raspberries,
blueberries, currants, and nuts from
the woods. They sewed clothes out
of soft deer hides and decorated
them with seashells, paint, feathers,
and dyed porcupine quills. Using
bows and arrows, the men hunted
deer, moose, beavers, and birds.
They also constructed canoes for
travel over water and speared fish
from the rivers and lakes.

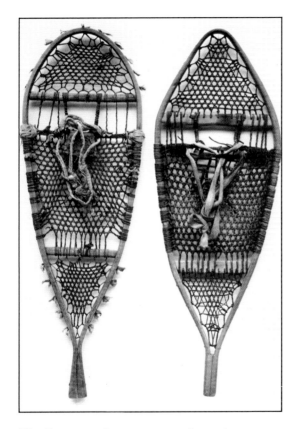

The Pennacook wove snowshoes from flexible branches and strips of leather.

During New Hampshire's chilling winters, the Indians wrapped themselves in warm furs. To travel easily across deep snow, they wore snowshoes. The men hunted wild game and went ice fishing for trout. The Indians also ate pemmican—a mixture of dried berries and smoked meats preserved for the cold season.

When spring arrived, the Pennacook tapped the sap from sugar maple trees, boiling it to make maple sugar and syrup. The Indians also watched the budding oak trees carefully. When the oak leaves were as big as a mouse's ear, the Pennacook knew it was time to plant corn.

21

European explorers first visited Pennacook territory in the early 1600s. King James I of Great Britain heard of the area's lush forests and its good fishing from John Smith, a British captain who had explored much of the Atlantic coast. The king claimed this land for Britain, and his son Prince Charles named it New England.

In 1621 King James granted a large chunk of New England to two wealthy noblemen, Captain John Mason and Sir Ferdinando Gorges. Several groups of British people went to live on the newly claimed land. The settlers built several villages, forming a **colony**, or settlement, which was ruled by Great Britain.

Mason and Gorges split up their land in 1629. Mason named his portion New Hampshire, after Hampshire County, his homeland in Britain. By 1640 the colony of New Hampshire had four towns —Portsmouth, Exeter, Dover, and Hampton.

Captain John Smith

In 1629 Mason and Gorges chose names for their properties. Mason's colony became New Hampshire and Gorges named his portion Maine.

New Hampshire's settlers traded British shirts, blankets, kettles, axes, and knives to the Indians for furs and fish. Ships carried the furs and dried fish back to Great Britain, where people were eager to buy them. The settlers also cut down rows and rows of trees. Shipbuilders used the colony's vast wood supply to make ships for Britain's navy.

With the help of Native Americans, New Hampshire's settlers began to feel at home. The Indians taught the settlers how to farm, how to catch wild game, and how to find plants that were good for eating and for making medicines.

But contact with the Europeans changed the Indians' way of life.

Beavers were hunted for their fur, which Europeans used to make hats.

The Pennacook grew dependent on trading with the settlers. By the late 1600s, the Indians had stopped making some of their own goods.

As the settlers' villages grew, New Hampshire's wilderness also changed. Settlers cut down more forests for lumber and to make room for farmland. Without trees and brush to live in, many wild animals fled to find new shelter. As a result, the Indians in New Hampshire had to travel farther to hunt game animals.

Sawdust from the colonists' lumber mills polluted the water in nearby rivers. Dams, or walls across rivers, had been built to form **reservoirs**—large pools of water—for everyday use. But the dams also slowed the water's flow, and many fish died in the dirty, slow-moving water. Soon there were fewer fish for the Pennacook to catch. The Indians grew angry about all of these changes.

By 1689 Great Britain had colonies along much of the Atlantic coast. The British also claimed

Because tree stumps were so difficult to remove, early colonists often planted their crops around them.

land west of these settlements, thinking they would find even more fish, furs, and lumber in the west.

25

Meanwhile, the French had established many trading posts to the north and to the west of New Hampshire. Like the British, the French made lots of money selling the furs they got from the Native Americans. The French wanted to control the fur trade throughout North America, and they were willing to fight the British for it.

PASSACONAWAY

Chief Passaconaway was a Pennacook sachem, or leader, in the 1600s. He, like many other Indians, caught a disease brought to America by the Europeans. These new diseases killed thousands of Indians. Only 1 out of every 20 Indians, mostly Pennacook, in New Hampshire and Vermont were spared from disease in the 1600s.

Even on his deathbed, Passaconaway was thinking about the future of his people. When the Indians began feuding with British colonists, the wise chief worried that a war would destroy the Pennacook. Passaconaway urged the Pennacook to keep peace with the settlers, but the battles that had begun did not end for many years.

By the late 1600s, French traders knew that many Native Americans were fighting mad at the British. Wanting the Indians on their side, the French encouraged them to attack British colonists. In response to the attacks, New Hampshire and other colonies offered a reward for the scalp of any Indian—man, woman, or child.

The series of battles involving the French, British, and Indians—called the French and Indian wars—finally ended in 1763 with a British victory. Many Pennacook had been killed in battle. Others had died from diseases they had caught from the colonists. The survivors fled to Canada, where French settlers were friendly to most Indians.

This fort in western New Hampshire has been restored to look like it did when the British used it during battles against the French and the Indians.

27

To help pay for the French and Indian wars, Great Britain raised taxes in its 13 North American colonies, including New Hampshire. The high taxes made the colonists very angry. The Americans did not like Britain telling them what to do, so they decided to fight for independence.

The war for independence, called the American Revolution, broke out in 1775. New Hampshire sent

New Hampshire's flag features the *Raleigh,* a warship built at Portsmouth for use in the revolutionary war.

The *Ranger,* constructed at Portsmouth, gained fame as the first U.S. ship to hoist the Stars and Stripes.

hundreds of men to Boston to fight the British soldiers. In January 1776, New Hampshire adopted its own **constitution,** or written set of laws. With this document, New Hampshire became the first colony to form a government separate from Great Britain.

After the colonies won the war in 1783, they wrote a constitution for the United States of America. On June 21, 1788, New Hampshire became the ninth state to sign the U.S. Constitution and join the new nation.

Workers in a blacksmith shop melt iron and pound it into horseshoes.

By this time, more than 140,000 settlers lived in New Hampshire. Many families had small farms, which were clustered around villages. Farmers cleared the land to plant fields of wheat, Indian corn, peas, pumpkins, and oats. Women spun yarn, wove cloth, and sewed the family's clothes. Families made soap from scratch, dipped their own candles, wove baskets and rugs, and sewed quilts.

In the villages, blacksmiths hammered away on nails, hooks, and horseshoes. Millers ground corn and wheat. Tanners prepared animal hides for leather shoes and saddles. Money was scarce, so townsfolk often bartered, or traded, for goods and services. For example, farmers might trade part of their corn crop to the miller in exchange for having the rest of the crop ground into cornmeal.

In the early 1800s, industries began to grow in New Hampshire. Settlers had learned to create **hydropower,** or energy from flowing water, by building dams across rivers. The dams held back the water, which was then released through large wheels. The force of the water was used to power machines in mills. Soon, cloth mills sprang up alongside the state's swift rivers and streams.

In the 1800s, town halls were built throughout New Hampshire, giving residents a place to hold town meetings.

As industry grew, transportation improved. In 1838 New Hampshire opened its first railroad. Trains began to transport goods to markets in other states. Railroads made it easy for lumber companies to reach the vast forests of New Hampshire's White Mountains. Crews of 30 men or more would camp among the trees, axing huge areas of forest before moving on.

Loggers floated timber down rivers or sent it by train to lumber and paper mills.

Many products went by train to Portsmouth, which had become a leading port and shipbuilding town. From Portsmouth, ships packed with U.S. products sailed to Europe. And ships from other countries docked at the busy port to unload their cargoes.

The Connecticut River served as a passageway for lumber from New Hampshire's northern woods.

The state's traders and manufacturers had Daniel Webster, a New Hampshire politician, to fight for laws in their favor. While working for the U.S. government, Webster influenced lawmakers, presidents, and judges. People throughout the United States listened to what he had to say.

Webster's most important struggle affected the entire nation. In the 1830s, some people wanted the states in the Union, or United States, to have laws more powerful than the nation's laws. But Webster fought for strong national laws, fearing that a weak U.S. government would not be able to hold the young country together.

By 1850 many Americans were worried about national unity. In the Southern states, many people used slaves from Africa to work in the fields and to do other hard work. In New Hampshire, as in all Northern states, slavery was illegal. When politicians tried to outlaw slavery throughout the nation, the Southern states threatened to leave the Union.

Daniel Webster

33

Daniel Webster was against slavery, but his main goal was to keep the nation together. Webster helped pass the Compromise of 1850, a series of laws about slavery that he hoped both Northerners and Southerners could agree on.

The Compromise of 1850 helped calm the nation for a while, but people continued to argue about slavery. In 1854 U.S. president Franklin Pierce, another New Hampshirite, signed a law permitting two new U.S. territories to decide for themselves if they wanted to allow slavery.

Whose Territory?

By 1854 the United States had claimed almost all of the territory between Mexico and Canada. As people moved west to buy land, questions arose about whether to allow slavery in new territories. Northerners wanted to outlaw slavery in the territories, but Southerners wanted it legalized. The Kansas-Nebraska Act of 1854 said that settlers in the two new territories could decide for themselves whether or not to permit slavery.

Northerners became very angry about the law, and arguments between the North and South grew into the Civil War (1861–1865). During this war, the Southern states formed a separate country and fought against the Northern states. The North won the war in 1865, and the nation was once again united.

In the 1800s, stone quarries, or mines, near Concord supplied tons of granite to builders.

These young French Canadians found work in a New Hampshire textile (cloth) mill in the late 1800s.

After the Civil War, New Hampshire's growing factories needed more and more workers. Thousands of **immigrants** from Europe and Canada came to New Hampshire for jobs. By 1874 more than half of New Hampshire's workers were employed in manufacturing. The state's products included everything from shoes and books to glass and pianos.

Industry boomed even more in 1917, when the United States entered World War I. To supply the soldiers, workers produced weapons, leather boots, and cloth for uniforms.

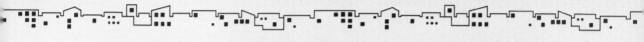

Manchester's Mammoth Mills

By the early 1900s, the Amoskeag Manufacturing Company in Manchester had become the largest textile factory in the world. At its peak, the company operated 30 mills and employed about 17,000 workers. The company owed its size in part to the unusual way it began. First, planners built rows and rows of mills below the Amoskeag Falls of the Merrimack River. The city of Manchester was then designed around the company's buildings.

Thousands of people moved to Manchester to find work in the growing company, bringing along their unique cloth-making skills. The Scots, for example, were experts at making gingham, or checkered cloth. Sometimes entire families worked in the mills. Young boys and girls often cleaned or ran the thread-making machines. Women were usually weavers or cloth inspectors, and men operated the heavy machinery. On busy days, the company's workers turned out more than 50 miles (80 km) of cloth per hour!

In the late 1920s, the Amoskeag Manufacturing Company began losing money. By 1936 the mills had closed down, leaving thousands of people jobless. Although it later recovered from the loss of the mills, the city of Manchester faced years of poverty. The cloth-making machines at the Amoskeag Company have been silent for many years. But the gigantic factory buildings still stand, reminding residents of Manchester's past.

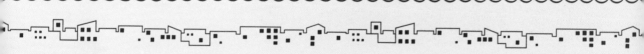

The town of Berlin in northern New Hampshire grew rapidly in the early 1900s. New railroads and paved roads for automobiles opened the north to vacationers.

Businesses throughout the United States suffered during the Great Depression of the 1930s. Many Americans lost their jobs and had very little money to spend. Because people could not afford to buy New Hampshire's products, factories in the state struggled to stay open.

The outbreak of World War II in 1939 gave a new boost to many U.S. businesses. Factories in New Hampshire again supplied the military with items such as parachutes, uniforms, weapons, and submarines. The state also sent many soldiers overseas to fight in the war.

After the war ended in 1945, New Hampshire advertised throughout the country, encouraging people to spend their vacations in the Granite State. More and more visitors traveled to New Hampshire to hike in the mountain forests and to sunbathe on the beaches. In the 1970s, new industries came to the state. Many New Hampshirites began to make computers and electrical parts.

Early computer systems could fill an entire room with equipment.

9,000 B.C.	American Indians move into what is now New Hampshire
A.D. 1614	Captain John Smith explores the New England coast for Britain
1629	John Mason gives New Hampshire its name
1763	The French and Indian wars end with a British victory
1788	New Hampshire becomes the ninth state
1800	Portsmouth begins making ships for the U.S. Navy
1850	Daniel Webster helps pass the Compromise of 1850

New Hampshirites once depended mainly on furs, fish, and lumber for survival. People in the state have since found new ways to make a living. The Granite State has become a center for modern technology, producing computer chips, electrical circuits, and machinery parts. New Hampshirites have shown that their determination to succeed is set in stone as hard as granite.

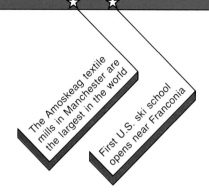

1920 — The Amoskeag textile mills in Manchester are the largest in the world

1929 — First U.S. ski school opens near Franconia

1990 — The Christa McAuliffe Planetarium opens

The Christa McAuliffe Planetarium *(right)* opened in Concord in 1990. McAuliffe *(inset)*, a schoolteacher from New Hampshire, was on board the space shuttle *Challenger* in 1986 when it exploded seconds after takeoff, killing all of the crew members.

41

Living and Working in New Hampshire

New Hampshire is one of the country's smallest states, and it has a small population to match its size. Just over one million people call New Hampshire home. Unlike the state's size, however, its population is growing.

Many New Hampshirites have ancestors who came from Great Britain during New Hampshire's days as a British colony. Some people trace their roots back to other European countries. One-fourth of New Hampshire's residents are descendants of French Canadians who moved to the United States in the 1800s. Latinos, African Americans, and Asian Americans make up about 1 percent of the state's population.

Slightly more than half of New Hampshire's residents live in cities, most of which are small. Manchester, New Hampshire's largest city, has about 100,000 people. Nashua, Portsmouth, Rochester, and Concord—the state capital—are the next four largest cities.

New Hampshire's cities and countryside offer many exciting things to see and do. Racing fans watch cars and motorcycles zip around the track at the New Hampshire International Speedway in Loudon. Champion dogs race at Seabrook Greyhound Park, and racehorses compete at Rockingham Park in Salem. During the winter, a handful of world skiing championships take place in the White Mountains. And in the summer, sailboats race in the Hobie Cat Regatta at Hampton Beach.

Young sliders look tired out after a long day on the slopes.

Lumberjack competitions test the muscles of New Hampshirites at fairs throughout the state.

New Hampshire's historical sites attract many modern explorers. In the center of Portsmouth, Strawbery Banke has been restored to look the way it did during its days as a colonial seaport. The Cog Railway, in the northern part of the state, takes brave riders up and down the hair-raising slopes of Mount Washington. There, visitors can see Old Peppersass—the first train used on the railway—and peek at the weather dials in the Sherman Adams Summit Building.

With hundreds of parks and forests, the Granite State is a perfect place for lovers of the great outdoors. Adventures range from scaling Mount Monadnock to camping at Moose Brook State Park. Photographers and hikers hope to spot some of the state's wildlife. Swift rivers, large lakes, and coastal waters test the skills of boaters, fishers, and swimmers. And during the cold season, snowmobilers and skiers plow through New Hampshire's deep snow.

New Hampshire's White Mountains can be a challenge for hikers.

A nature-study class *(below)* listens to a recording of an owl's call. A sailboarder *(right)* makes waves on Little Dublin Pond.

These outdoor attractions make tourism a big business in New Hampshire. Besides crowds of local vacationers, more than four million people visit the state each year. Thousands of New Hampshirites have service jobs, working to assist visitors in parks and resorts. Workers also serve as guides, innkeepers, and waitpeople.

A school bus passes through one of New Hampshire's covered bridges. Bus drivers provide a service to students throughout the state.

Besides helping tourists, service workers in New Hampshire sell everyday products such as food, clothing, and gasoline. Doctors, teachers, bankers, and mechanics provide other important services to people in New Hampshire. Government workers at the state's weather research center atop Mount Washington sell weather information to the National Weather Service, to the U.S. Army, and to engineers around the nation. Altogether, more than half of the state's workers have some type of service job.

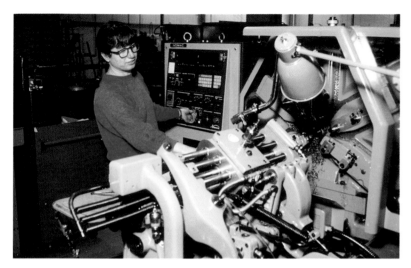

Manufacturers in New Hampshire make everything from ball bearings *(left)* to barrels *(below)*.

One of every four jobholders in New Hampshire works in manufacturing. Unlike the factories of the past, many of the state's modern industries specialize in high technology. Many New Hampshirites put together computers, design computer software, or make parts for machines and military equipment. Leather and plastic products also are made in the state.

The state's many craftsworkers take pride in producing handmade items much like those made in colonial days. Lamps, jewelry, rugs, wicker baskets, pottery, quilts, and pewter candlesticks fill shops throughout the state. New Hampshirites also make and sell fresh maple syrup, jellies, and relishes.

Maple tree sap is used to make sweet syrups and candies.

A potter shapes a clay vase.

50

Construction workers make use of the state's supply of lumber and rock.

New Hampshire's forests provide the raw material for wooden products and paper goods. Loggers cut down trees and haul the wood to lumber and paper mills. Much of the wood is sawed into lumber for building houses and making furniture. At paper mills, machines roll out writing paper and process paper bags and paper towels. Other workers print magazines and newspapers.

Some mining still goes on in New Hampshire. Miners scoop up sand, crush stones into gravel, and carve granite from the state's mountains and hills. Sand and gravel are used for making roads and concrete. The granite is shipped throughout the United States to be used in construction.

51

In the late 1800s, half the people who lived in New Hampshire farmed the land. Nowadays only 2 percent of the state's workers earn a living from farming. Most farmers raise dairy cows, but some have beef cattle, hogs, and poultry. Farmers grow more hay than any other crop, using it to feed New Hampshire's cattle. Some farmers

Some farmers in New Hampshire grow Christmas trees.

specialize in apples, the state's leading fruit crop.

Tourism, high-tech industry, logging, and farming are just a few of the ways New Hampshirites earn money. Residents of the Granite State are proud of what they have accomplished.

Young New Hampshirites enjoy a parade.

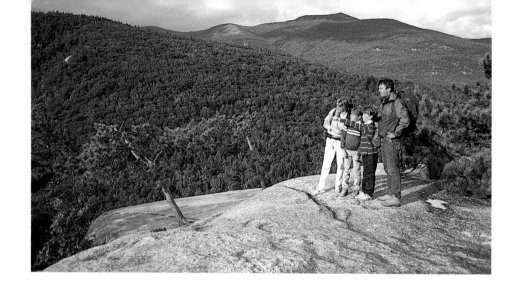

Protecting the Environment

For hundreds of years, New Hampshire's population grew very slowly. In 1950, after more than 160 years of statehood, only 500,000 people lived in New Hampshire.

But by 1980, the state's population had doubled. And though New Hampshire has fewer residents per square mile than many other states do, its population is on the rise.

New Hampshire's fresh air, scenic countryside, sparkling rivers, and abundant forests have begun to attract more people than ever before. The newcomers provide New Hampshire with more workers, who help the state earn more money. But a higher population can also threaten the state's environment.

Many people *(lower left)* **come to New Hampshire to enjoy the outdoors. But more people create more garbage** *(below),* **which causes overflowing landfills.**

During the mid-1980s alone, new homes, factories, roads, and office buildings swallowed up 20,000 acres (8,094 hectares) of New Hampshire's forests and farmland a year. These built-up areas, or **developments**, spread out over more and more land, increasing air pollution and

Within two years, construction workers turned the pasture into a housing development.

garbage in the state. Worried about losing the state's wilderness and countryside areas, New Hampshirites began looking for ways to keep some of the land clean and unspoiled.

From 1986 to 1992, New Hampshire managed a program to help preserve some of the land by protecting it from more new development. Millions of dollars from the state, from cities, and from businesses and individuals helped support the program. The money was used to pay landowners to sign a contract, or agreement, promising not to build or make major changes on the land.

The contracts prevent landowners from putting up new buildings, roads, or mines on lands that are protected. And the agreements also make certain areas open to the public for activities such as hiking, picnicking, and birdwatching. If the owner ever sells the land, the buyer must also agree to rules in the contract.

New condominiums and ski areas attract more and more vacationers to the mountains each winter.

Contracts now preserve more than 100,000 acres (40,470 hectares) of the state's forests, parks, lakeshores, and farmlands. Because New Hampshire's landscape varies from one place to another, each contract has different rules. On farmland, for example, a typical contract allows the owner to use the land for farming but not for new development.

Because more than 85 percent of the state is forested, many of the contracts are on forests. The rules in these contracts protect woodlands in many ways. Some rules ban motor vehicles, which damage the soft floor of the forest. Others forbid mining on the land.

But contracts on forests do allow logging. New Hampshire's lumber

industry adds about $1.5 billion to the state's earnings each year. Many landowners would have refused to sign a contract if it kept them from using this valuable natural resource.

Farming *(facing page)* and logging *(left)* are allowed on most lands preserved by contracts. Loggers supply lumber for many industries, including the paper mills *(right)* in Berlin, New Hampshire.

Young New Hampshirites learn about trees and the homes they provide for wildlife.

Some New Hampshirites feel that the contract program is not enough to save the state's woodlands. Many of these citizens work on projects to help control the type, amount, and location of trees cut down in New Hampshire's forests. And they try to make sure that enough new trees are planted to replace those cut down by loggers. Some residents, concerned about losing the wooded habitats of New Hampshire's birds and animals, would like to end logging in much of the state.

New Hampshirites are also teaching their children to take care of the Granite State's land, hoping to preserve it far into the future. By working together, the state's residents can tackle the challenge of caring for the land as more and more people move into the state. The Old Man of the Mountains—watching over the state with his granite stare—reminds New Hampshirites of the beauty of the state they are proud to call home.

A group of students measures the growth of trees in a wooded area near Antrim, New Hampshire.

New Hampshire's Famous People

ARTISTS

Daniel French (1850–1931), from Exeter, New Hampshire, is remembered for his statues, including *The Minute Man of Concord*, honoring American heroes. One of his most famous statues is *Abraham Lincoln*, which stands in the Lincoln Memorial in Washington, D.C.

Maxfield Parrish (1870–1966) illustrated hundreds of magazines and books including *Mother Goose in Prose* and *The Arabian Nights*. The scenic area around Cornish, New Hampshire, where Parrish lived for much of his life, inspired many of his works.

◄ DANIEL FRENCH

MAXFIELD PARRISH ►

ALAN SHEPARD, JR. ►

ASTRONAUT

Alan Shepard, Jr. (born 1923), rocketed into space in 1961, becoming the first U.S. astronaut. In 1971 he commanded the *Apollo 14* for the third moon landing in history and became the fifth astronaut to walk on the moon. Shepard is from East Derry, New Hampshire.

ATHLETES

Barbara Ann Cochran (born 1951) is a skier from Claremont, New Hampshire. Cochran won a gold medal for the women's slalom, a zigzag skiing event, in the 1972 Olympic Games.

62

Mike Flanagan (born 1951) pitched for the Baltimore Orioles from 1975 to 1987, when he moved to the Toronto Blue Jays. In 1979 Flanagan won more baseball games than any other pitcher in the American League and won the Cy Young Award. Flanagan grew up in Manchester, New Hampshire.

Red Rolfe (1908–1969), from Pennacook, New Hampshire, played and coached professional baseball. As the third baseman for the New York Yankees, Rolfe led the American League in 1939 with 213 hits and 139 runs.

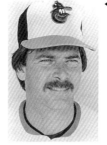
◀ MIKE FLANAGAN

RED ROLFE ▶

BOB MONTANA ▶

▲ MARY BAKER EDDY

HORACE GREELEY ▶

CARTOONIST

Bob Montana (1920–1975) created the comic strip "Archie" in 1942. The cartoons described the lives of American teenagers. Many of Montana's characters were based on classmates from his high school in Manchester.

EDUCATORS & JOURNALISTS

Mary Baker Eddy (1821–1910) founded the Christian Science religion in 1879. In 1908 she started the daily newspaper, *The Christian Science Monitor*. Eddy was born in Bow, New Hampshire.

Horace Greeley (1811–1872), from Amherst, New Hampshire, founded and published The *New York Tribune*, a famous newspaper in the 1800s. In the paper, Greeley voiced his ideas and became an important political influence in America.

Sarah Josepha Hale (1788–1879) from Newport, New Hampshire, wrote and edited *Ladies' Magazine* and *Godey's Lady's Book*. The magazines stressed pride and education for women. Hale also wrote several books and the nursery rhyme, "Mary Had a Little Lamb."

◄ SARAH JOSEPHA HALE

INVENTOR

Earl Tupper (1907–1983) began selling his plastic storage containers to stores in 1945. Tupperware did not become popular until the 1950s, however, when sales skyrocketed at home parties. Tupper was born in Berlin, New Hampshire.

EARL TUPPER ►

▲ FRANKLIN PIERCE

LEADERS

Elizabeth Gurley Flynn (1890–1964), from Concord, New Hampshire, helped factory workers throughout the United States gain more rights and better working conditions. Flynn also helped found the American Civil Liberties Union, an organization dedicated to protecting the rights of all Americans.

Kancamagus (1655?–1691?) was the last chief of the Pennacook Indians in New Hampshire. When war broke out between the British and the Indians, Kancamagus led his people to Canada to escape attacks. A highway in New Hampshire following that route is named after him.

Franklin Pierce (1804–1869), the fourteenth president of the United States, was born in Hillsboro, New Hampshire. One of Pierce's nicknames was Young Hickory of the Granite Hills.

Salmon P. Chase (1808–1873), from Cornish, New Hampshire, was secretary of the U.S. Treasury when in 1863 he issued the first "greenbacks," or green dollar bills. He became the chief justice of the U.S. Supreme Court the next year. Chase often defended runaway slaves and supported giving free land to settlers in the West.

◀ SALMON P. CHASE

ALICE BROWN ▶

WRITERS

Alice Brown (1856–1948) wrote short stories and plays describing the people and places of New Hampshire. Her works include *Meadow-grass: Tales of New England* and *Children of Earth.* Brown was born in Hampton Falls, New Hampshire.

Robert Frost (1874–1963) attended Dartmouth College in Hanover, New Hampshire, and later lived on farms in Derry and Franconia, New Hampshire. Frost wrote poems that celebrate nature and daily life in New England.

Eleanor Porter (1868–1920), a children's author from Littleton, New Hampshire, wrote her way to fame with *Pollyanna.* The popular story sold over one million copies and was later translated into many languages.

J. D. Salinger (born 1919) lives near Cornish, New Hampshire. The author of many short stories, Salinger is probably most famous for his novel, *Catcher in the Rye.* The book is about the problems a teenage boy faces while growing up.

◀ ROBERT FROST

65

Facts-at-a-Glance

Nickname: Granite State
Song: "Old New Hampshire"
Motto: Live Free or Die
Flower: purple lilac
Tree: white birch
Bird: purple finch

Population: 1,109,252*
Rank in population, nationwide: 40th
Area: 9,351 sq mi (24,312 sq km)
Rank in area, nationwide: 46th
Date and ranking of statehood:
   June 21, 1788, the 9th state
Capital: Concord
Major cities (and populations*):
   Manchester (99,567), Nashua (79,662),
   Concord (36,006), Rochester (26,630),
   Portsmouth (25,925)
U.S. senators: 2
U.S. representatives: 2
Electoral votes: 4

Places to visit: Polar Caves Park near Plymouth, Science Center of New Hampshire in Holderness, Wildcat Mountain near Pinkham Notch, Lost River in North Woodstock, Story Land in Glen

Annual events: World Championship Sled Dog Derby in Laconia (Feb.), Monadnock Balloon and Aviation Festival on Mount Monadnock (June), Children's Festival in Hampton Beach (Aug.), World Mud Bowl in North Conway (Sept.), Northern Lights Festival in Waterville Valley (Nov.)

* 1990 census

| Average January temperature: 19° F (−7° C) | Average July temperature: 68° F (20° C) |

Natural resources: forests, lakes, rivers, granite, feldspar, soil, clay, sand, gravel

Agricultural products: milk, apples, berries, eggs, poultry, beef cattle, maple syrup, hay, Christmas trees

Manufactured goods: computers, electric lamps, electronics equipment, paper products, lumber and wood products, plastics, leather, metals

ENDANGERED SPECIES
Mammals—lynx, small-footed myotis
Birds—bald eagle, golden eagle, peregrine falcon, pied-billed grebe, piping plover, loggerhead shrike, Henslow's sparrow, common tern, sedge wren
Reptiles—timber rattlesnake
Fish—short-nosed sturgeon, Sunapee trout
Plants—robbin's cinquefoil, small whorled pogonia, Gesup's milk vetch

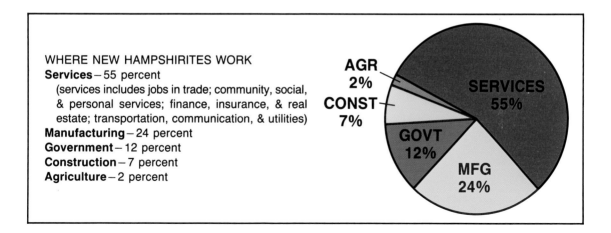

WHERE NEW HAMPSHIRITES WORK
Services—55 percent
(services includes jobs in trade; community, social, & personal services; finance, insurance, & real estate; transportation, communication, & utilities)
Manufacturing—24 percent
Government—12 percent
Construction—7 percent
Agriculture—2 percent

AGR 2%
CONST 7%
SERVICES 55%
GOVT 12%
MFG 24%

67

PRONUNCIATION GUIDE

Amoskeag (am-uh-SKAY-uhg)

Androscoggin (an-druh-SKAWG-uhn)

Exeter (EHK-suht-ur)

Gorges, Ferdinando (GOR-jehz, fir-dih-NAHN-doh)

Monadnock (muh-NAD-nahk)

Nashua (NASH-uh-wuh)

Pemigewasset (pehm-ih-juh-WAHS-uht)

Pennacook (PEHN-uh-kook)

Piscataqua (pihs-KAT-uh-kwaw)

Portsmouth (PORT-smuth)

Winnipesaukee (wihn-uh-puh-SAW-kee)

Glossary

colony   A territory ruled by a country some distance away.

constitution   The system of basic laws or rules of a government, society, or organization. The document in which these laws or rules are written.

development   The buildup of homes, office buildings, factories, and roads upon land that once was wild. Human activities, such as mining and logging, that remove things from the land also are types of development.

glacier   A large body of ice and snow that moves slowly over land.

hydropower   The electricity produced by using the force of flowing water. Also called hydroelectric power.

immigrant   A person who moves into a foreign country and settles there.

lava   Hot, melted rock that erupts from a volcano or from cracks in the earth's surface and that hardens as it cools.

precipitation   Rain, snow, hail, and other forms of moisture that fall to earth.

reservoir   A place where water is collected and stored for later use.

Index

71

Acknowledgments:

Maryland Cartographics, Inc., pp. 2, 10; Tony LaGruth, pp. 2–3, 9, 13 (right); George Karn, p. 6; Craig Blouin, pp. 7, 15, 43, 44, 45, 47 (left), 51, 55 (left), 56, 57, 58, 59 (left and right), 68; © John D. Cunningham / Visuals Unlimited, pp. 8, 27; Jim Simondet, p. 11; David Brownell / State of New Hampshire, pp. 12, 54; © Gerry Lemmo, pp. 13 (left), 17 (full page), 18, 24, 47 (right), 48, 71; © Makonny T. Titlow / Visuals Unlimited, p. 14; Meade Cadot, Harris Center for Conservation Education, pp. 16, 61; © Will Troyer / Visuals Unlimited, p. 17 (inset); U.S. Fish & Wildlife Service, p. 19; Hillel Burger, Peabody Museum, Harvard University, p. 20; National Museum of the American Indian / Smithsonian Institution, neg. no. 14656, p. 21; Virginia State Library and Archives, p. 22; New Hampshire Historical Society, pp. 23, #F411, 26, #G790, 29, #F3551, 35, #G370, 38, #N14HS242; Independent Picture Service, pp. 25, 30, 33; © James Blank / Root Resources, p. 31; Dartmouth College Library, pp. 32, 39, 62 (top right), 63 (top right); Museum of American Textile History, p. 36; Lynn Rice, p. 41 (above); NASA, pp. 41 (below), 62 (bottom); © John Kohout / Root Resources, p. 46; MPB Corporation, Keene, NH, p. 49 (left); Sharon Callahan, League of New Hampshire Craftsmen, p. 49 (right); B. Alexander, League of New Hampshire Craftsmen, p. 50 (left); New Hampshire Department of Agriculture, pp. 50 (right), 52; State of New Hampshire, p. 53; New Hampshire Department of Environmental Services, p. 55 (right); New Hampshire Fish and Game, p. 60; Library of Congress, p. 62 (top left), 63 (center left), 63 (bottom), 64 (bottom), 65 (top); National Baseball Library, Cooperstown, NY, p. 63 (top left); Montana Family, p. 63 (center right); Dictionary of American Portraits, p. 64 (top left); Tupperware Home Parties, p. 64 (top right); Boston Athenaeum, p. 65 (center); Courtesy of the Jones Library, Inc., Amherst, MA, Reprinted by permission of the Estate of Robert Frost, p. 65 (bottom).